2-50

M000192437

YOU M **1934** THIS

MILESTONES, MEMORIES,
TRIVIA AND FACTS, NEWS EVENTS,
PROMINENT PERSONALITIES &
SPORTS HIGHLIGHTS OF THE YEAR

TO : _____

FROM : _____

MESSAGE : _____

_____

*selected and researched
by
betsy dexter*

WARNER ⦿ TREASURES™

PUBLISHED BY WARNER BOOKS

A TIME WARNER COMPANY

Warner Books, Inc.
1271 Avenue of the Americas
New York, New York 10020

Warner Treasures is a
trademark of Warner Books, Inc.

A Time Warner Company

DESIGN:
CAROL BOKUNIEWICZ DESIGN
PRINTED IN SINGAPORE
FIRST PRINTING: SEPTEMBER 1996
10 9 8 7 6 5 4 3 2 1
ISBN: 0-446-91146-1

It was the year FDR declared that the New Deal was here to stay. The Civil Works Administration provided employment for 4 million, and hundreds of thousands of young men signed up for the Civilian Conservation Corps, which fed them, sheltered them, and paid a monthly rate of $30 to build roads, construct flood control systems, help with reforestation, and fight forest fires. In further anti-Depression maneuvers, the president devalued the dollar to 60 cents, set up the Federal Housing Administration, and established the Federal Farm Mortgage Corporation.

THE DIONNE QUINTUPLETS WERE BORN IN ONTARIO, CANADA. THE FIVE GIRLS, WHO SOON CAPTURED EVERYONE'S HEARTS, WERE THE FIRST KNOWN QUINTS TO SURVIVE.

They called it a "black blizzard" when 300 tons of Plains states topsoil blew away. The Dust Bowl resulted in a massive migration to the West.

Alcatraz, an island across the bay from San Francisco, was made a federal maximum security prison.

Chemist Wallace Carothers produced polymer 66, later known as **nylon.**

newsreel

SHOCK WAVES WENT THROUGH THE SOCIAL REGISTER WHEN A NEW YORK COURT RULED MRS. GLORIA MORGAN VANDERBILT UNFIT FOR CUSTODY OF HER DAUGHTER, GLORIA VANDERBILT, THE TEN-YEAR-OLD WITH THE $2.8 MILLION TRUST FUND.

Mrs. Vanderbilt, Gloria, and her aunt, Mrs. Harry Payne Whitney

War erupted in East Africa, as Italians and Ethiopians battled over a disputed area on the border of Italian Somaliland.

international

Chiang Kai-Shek

headlines

IN GERMANY, ADOLF HITLER COMBINED THE OFFICES OF CHANCELLOR AND PRESIDENT, THEN GAVE HIMSELF THE TITLE OF FÜHRER, WHICH LITERALLY TRANSLATES AS "LEADER."

In France, the Stavisky Affair, a high-level financial scandal, caused right-wing riots and forced the resignation of two successive French premiers of the ruling left-wing coalition.

MAO TSE-TUNG

The Red Army, under Mao Tse-tung, withstood attacks by the Chinese Nationalist Army under Chiang Kai-shek. Mao led his army on the famous Long March, a 6,000-mile trek that extended from south to north China. More than two-thirds of the marchers died in battle during the trek.

el Capp

Cartoonist Al Capp created the comic strip *Li'l Abner*, introducing American readers to the denizens of Dogpatch.

RETROSPECTIVES OF THE ART OF GEORGIA O'KEEFFE AND SALVADOR DALÍ OPENED IN NEW YORK.

In Rome, Benito Mussolini ordered all teachers to wear Fascist uniforms at school.

cultural
milestones

Post-Prohibition, purchases of Coca-Cola soft drinks took a nosedive.

In Berlin, the Nazis ordered new music to replace Jewish composer Felix Mendelssohn's score for *A Midsummer Night's Dream*.

The Sears & Roebuck catalog began to list contraceptive devices.

The Utopian Society was incorporated in Los Angeles. The Society used chain letters to tell citizens that profit was the root of all evil.

Radio Guide's Popularity Poll Winners

1. Amos 'n' Andy
2. Burns and Allen
3. Myrt and Marge
4. Joe Penner
5. Bing Crosby
6. Rudy Vallee
7. Jack Benny
8. Eddie Cantor
9. Ben Bernie
10. Wayne King and His Orchestra

Thanks to Joe Penner, a kooky and popular radio comedian, Americans went around saying "You nasty man!" and "Wanna buy a duck?"

top new shows

1. "The Bob Hope Show"
2. "Kraft Music Hall,"
   hosted by Bing Crosby
3. "Hollywood Hotel,"
   hosted by Dick Powell and Louella Parsons
4. "The Palmolive Beauty Box Theatre,"
   featuring Jessica Dragonette, and Fanny Brice as "Baby Snooks"
5. "Major Bowes and His Original Amateur Hour"

Bob Hope

DIVORCE

Philosopher **Bertrand Russell,** 62, was divorced by **Countess Dora Russell,** in London, on the grounds of adultery. **Anna Roosevelt Dall,** daughter of President Franklin Roosevelt, was divorced from **Curtis Bean Dall** in the town of Minden, just outside Reno, NV.

DOROTHY PARKER AND ALAN CAMPBELL

weddings of the year

Dorothy Parker, 40, *New Yorker* scribe and Algonquin Round Table wit, married actor **Alan Campbell,** 26, in Westbury, Long Island.

Stan Laurel, half of Laurel and Hardy, married **Ruth Rogers** in Agua Caliente, Mexico.

Wanda Toscanini, 25, daughter of conductor Arturo Toscanini, married pianist **Vladimir Horowitz,** 29, in Mila

DEATHS

Marie Curie, the first chemist to receive two Nobel Prizes, died in Valence, France, July 4, at the age of 66.

John Dillinger, Public Enemy Number One, was fatally shot by FBI man Melvin Purvis after seeing *Manhattan Melody* at the Biograph Theatre in Chicago, IL, July 22. He was 32.

milestones

celebrity births

Bonnie Parker and Clyde Barrow, outlaw lovers who terrorized the southwest in a two-year crime spree that left 12 dead, were gunned down by Texas Rangers May 23 in Gibsland, LA. Bonnie was 23; Clyde was 25.

Japanese naval hero **Heihachiro Togo** died May 30 in Tokyo, Japan.

Gloria Steinem, feminist, ex–Playboy bunny, and founder of *Ms. Magazine*, was born March 25 in Toledo, OH.

Sophia Loren, Oscar-winning actress, was born in Rome, Italy, September 20.

Hank Aaron, baseball Hall of Famer and all-time home-run record-holder, was born February 5 in Mobile, AL.

Carl Sagan, the world's best-known TV astronomer, was born November 9 in New York City.

Roberto Clemente, legendary Pittsburgh Pirate outfielder, was born in Carolina, Puerto Rico, August 18.

Billboard printed its first weekly survey of the most played songs on network radio, and *Down Beat*, the nation's premier jazz magazine, was founded.

'34

1. **the old spinning wheel** Ray Noble
2. **smoke gets in your eyes** Paul Whiteman
3. **let's fall in love** Eddy Duchin
4. **my little grass shack in kealakekua, hawaii** Ted Fio Rito
5. **the carioca** Enric Madriguera
6. **wagon wheels** Paul Whiteman
7. **little dutch mill** Bing Crosby
8. **cocktails for two** Duke Ellington
9. **i'll string along with you** Ted Fio Rito
10. **moonglow** Benny Goodman

hit music

On his National Biscuit radio show, "Let's Dance," Benny Goodman brought swing to large audiences. The band featured legendary players like Bunny Berrigan, Jess Stacy, and Gene Krupa on drums. Arrangements were handled by Fletcher Henderson.

BENNY GOODMAN

1. **anthony adverse**
   hervey allen

2. **lamb in his bosom**
   caroline miller

3. **so red the rose**
   stark young

4. **good-bye, mr. chips**
   james hilton

5. **within this present**
   margaret ayer barnes

6. **work of art**
   sinclair lewis

7. **private worlds**
   phillis bottome

8. **mary peters**
   mary ellen chase

9. **oil for the lamps of china**
   alice tisdale hobart

10. **seven gothic tales**
    isak dinesen

Some readers were shocked—some were delighted—by the appearance this year of **Henry Miller's** *Tropic of Cancer*, a hysterically funny, sexually explicit work that shattered the boundaries of contemporary good taste.

James Cain published *The Postman Always Rings Twice*, the brooding novel destined to become a film-noir classic when it hit the screen.

books

nonfiction

1. **while rome burns**
   alexander woollcott

2. **life begins at forty**
   walter b. pitkin

3. **nijinsky**
   romola nijinsky

4. **100,000,000 guinea pigs**
   arthur kallet and f. j. schlink

5. **the native's return**
   louis adamic

6. **stars fell on alabama**
   carl carmer

7. **brazilian adventure**
   peter fleming

8. **forty-two years in the white house**
   ike hoover

9. **you must relax**
   edmund jacobson

10. **the life of our lord**
    charles dickens

IN AUTO RACING, SPEEDSTER **BILL CUMMINGS** OUTRACED THE FIELD AT A BLAZING 104.9 MILES PER HOUR TO WIN THE INDY 500.

Athlete Babe Didrikson took up golf this year. When asked if there was anything she *didn't* play, she replied, "Yeah, dolls."

In baseball, the St. Louis Cardinals took the World Series, blanking the Detroit Tigers, 11–0, in the seventh game.

IN PHILADELPHIA, NAVY TRIUMPHED OVER ARMY IN THEIR ANNUAL GRIDIRON MATCH-UP. THE 3–0 WIN MARKED THE FIRST NAVY VICTORY IN 10 YEARS.

In Pasadena, Columbia shut out Stanford at the Rose Bowl, 7–0.

FRED PERRY

sports

AT WIMBLEDON, IT WAS FRED PERRY OVER JACK CRAWFORD 6–3, 6–0, 7–5, AND DOROTHY ROUND OVER HELEN JACOBS 6–2, 5–7, 6–3.

In the All-Star game, National League pitcher Carl Hubbell of New York achieved the impossible. He struck out, in succession, Babe Ruth, Lou Gehrig, Jimmie Foxx, Al Simmons, and Joe Cronin—the most feared hitters in the game.

THE THIN MAN

The first of the *Thin Man* series appeared this year. The perpetually suave detective and his wife, played by William Powell and Myrna Loy, did more for the martini than all the bartenders in America.

It was a clean sweep for *It Happened One Night* this year at the Oscars. The film was so popular that the male undershirt business went into a major slump after Clark Gable took off his shirt and revealed a naked chest.

memorable films

Treasure Island, starring Wallace Beery and Freddie Bartholomew
The Count of Monte Cristo, starring Robert Donat
The Scarlet Pimpernel, starring Leslie Howard and Merle Oberon
Cleopatra, starring Claudette Colbert, a Cecil B. DeMille epic
Twentieth Century, a Howard Hawks film, starring John Barrymore and Carole Lombard
Imitation of Life, starring Claudette Colbert and Warren William
The Gay Divorcee, starring Fred Astaire and Ginger Rogers

IT HAPPENED ONE NIGHT

movies

oscar winners

Best Picture: **It Happened One Night**

Best Director: **Frank Capra, It Happened One Night**

Best Actress: **Claudette Colbert, It Happened One Night**

Best Actor: **Clark Gable, It Happened One Night**

Best Screenplay: **Robert Riskin, It Happened One Night**

Celebrating its 23rd anniversary, Chevrolet produced its 10 millionth car.

Several carmakers offered radio controls built into the dashboard. A controlled-current generator was offered to keep the battery charged.

'34

wheels

REO introduced a completely automatic transmission.

The Duesenberg SJ was the last car Fred Duesenberg designed before he died in a car accident. The vehicle featured a centrifugal supercharger, boosting the engine to 320 horsepower and a top speed of 129 miles per hour. Following industry trends, the custom bodies on the $9,500 Duesenberg chassis featured the modern, streamlined look.

Streamlining was stressed in the new DeSoto and Chrysler Airflow models. The Hupmobile and La Salle also featured the new aerodynamic emphasis.

ARTISTS SALVADOR DALÍ AND JEAN COCTEAU DESIGNED FANTASY PRINTS AND BUTTONS SHAPED LIKE FISH, STARS, AND CIRCUS HORSES FOR DESIGNER SCHIAPARELLI.

fashion

Ready-to-wear was the key phrase from Chanel. This collection sported a jersey jacket and easy skirt. The desired look was low-key elegance.

Shoulders were padded and extra wide. Some women preferred them covered with gold embroidery.

It was a big year for skimpy sportswear. A passion for outdoor sports—up to and including nudism—took over the nation. In bathing suits the look was backless and slashed.

Women wore hats on the side of their heads.

REALLY STYLISH WOMEN WENT WITH ROUGE, NAIL POLISH, AND RED LIP-STICK THIS YEAR. MOST MAKEUP WAS FESTIVE AND BRIGHT.

Cocktail lounges,

most furnished with jukeboxes, are the only type of major new construction in the country.

final factoid

archive photos: inside front cover, pages 1, 23, 25, inside back cover

associated press: pages 2, 3, 4, 5, 6, 10, 16, 17

photofest: pages 9, 13, 18, 19

gaslight: page 21

photo research:
alice albert

coordination:
rustyn birch

design:
carol bokuniewicz design
tony payne

'34